# NARRATIVE THERAPY

Unlocking Resilience, A Comprehensive Guide To Targeting Transformative Stories For Healing, Explore Key Concepts, Enhance Focus, And Achieve Therapeutic Success

## DR. WANDA MENDENHALL

**DISCLAIMER**

This book is the result of the author's own expertise, insight, and experience in the area of treatment. The author has no affiliation with any particular firm, business, or person mentioned in this

2

article. The content in this book is based exclusively on the author's knowledge and should not be construed as professional advice or a replacement for professional treatment or counseling.

Readers are recommended to seek professional counsel or guidance based on their unique circumstances or requirements. The author and publisher are not liable for any actions done in reliance on the information included in this book. Every person's circumstance is unique, so what works for one person may not work for another.

This book attempts to provide insights and knowledge for both education and personal growth.

The author does not recommend any certain therapy strategy or practice over another. Readers should exercise caution and check with trained specialists before using any knowledge or strategies discussed in this book.

By reading this book, the reader understands and accepts that the author and publisher are not accountable for any direct or indirect repercussions, damages, or losses that occur from the use or misuse of the material included herein.

# Table of Contents


INTRODUCTION.................................................12

CHAPTER ONE ...............................................16

Unraveling The Tapestry Of Narrative Therapy ......16

Embracing The Narrative Paradigm ......................16

Historical Roots And Evolution .............................17

Theoretical Foundations.....................................19

CHAPTER TWO ..............................................22

The Power Of Storytelling...................................22

Understanding Narratives ...................................22

Narrative Identity And Self-Construction ..............23

Cultural And Social Influences On Storytelling .......25

CHAPTER THREE ............................................28

Narrative Therapy Techniques And Tools...............28

Externalizing Problems .......................................28

Reauthoring Narratives .......................................30

Unique Outcomes And Exceptions.........................31

The Use Of Questions In Narrative Practices..........32

Influences Of Culture And Society On Storytelling .33

CHAPTER FOUR ..............................................36

Conversations That Heal.....................................36

The Therapeutic Dialogue ........................................36

Listening With Purpose...........................................38

Co-Creating New Narratives ...................................39

CHAPTER FIVE ........................................................42

Narrative Therapy In Action...................................42

Case Studies And Success Stories ..........................43

1. A Case of Resilience in Narrative Reframing ...43

2. Narrative Interventions and Family Dynamics 44

3. Identity Exploration: A Self-Discovery Journey

.................................................................................44

Applications In Different Settings ..........................45

1. Fostering Learning Narratives in Educational

Settings .................................................................45

2. Redefining Professional Narratives in the

Workplace .........................................................46

3. Empowering Collective Narratives Through

Community-Based Initiatives .............................46

Challenges And Ethical Considerations .................47

1. Neutrality and Advocacy in Balance ..............47

2. In Group Situations, Confidentiality ..............47

3. Cultural Awareness and Diversity...................48

CHAPTER SIX ................................................................50

Collaborative Approaches In Narrative Therapy.....50

The Role Of Collaboration In Change .....................51

1. Narratives in Common: ...................................51

2. Power Relationships: ......................................51

3. Externalizing Issues:......................................52

Involving Families And Support Systems................53

1. Systemic Viewpoint: ......................................53

2. Rewriting Family Stories: ...............................54

3. Considerations for Culture: ............................54

Interdisciplinary Collaboration ...........................55

1. Holistic Treatment: ........................................55

2. Information Exchange: ....................................56

3. Treatment Strategy:........................................56

CHAPTER SEVEN .................................................58

Integrating Cultural Competence...........................58

Cultural Sensitivity In Narrative Therapy ...............59

1. Recognizing Cultural Sensitivity:.....................59

2. Opportunities and Challenges: .......................59

3. Intersectionality:...........................................60

Addressing Diversity And Inclusivity .....................60

1. Cultural Competence Education: ......................60

2. Including Cultural Narratives:..........................61

3. Exploration in Collaboration: ........................61

Tailoring Approaches To Cultural Contexts ..........62

1. Formalization of Culture: ...............................62

2. Genograms of Culture:....................................62

3. Technique Flexibility:......................................63

CHAPTER EIGHT....................................................66

Narrative Therapy And Trauma ...........................66

Trauma-Informed Narrative Practices...................67

2. Externalizing the issue: ..................................68

3. Reauthoring the Narrative: ............................68

4. Cultural Sensitivity:........................................69

Resilience And Post-Traumatic Growth.................69

1. Identifying Strengths:.....................................70

2. Reframing problems: ......................................70

3. Creating a Preferred Narrative: ......................71

Case Examples Of Trauma Narratives ..................71

1. Surviving Domestic abuse: .............................71

2. A Combat Veteran's Journey:..........................72

3. Childhood Trauma and Resilience: ..................72

CHAPTER NINE .....................................................74

Research And Advances In Narrative Therapy........74

Current Research Findings ...................................74

    1. Narrative Therapy and Neuroscience: ...........74

    2. Adaptation to Culture and Effectiveness: .......75

    3. Specific Population Efficacy:............................76

Innovations In Narrative Techniques ...................77

    1. Integration of Digital and Technological Resources: ............................................................77

    2. Integrating Expressive Arts with Narrative: ....78

    3. Practices of Collaborative Narrative: ..............78

Future Directions In The Field ............................79

    1. Positive Psychology Integration: ...................79

    2. Globalization and Cultural Sensitivity:...........80

    3. Further Investigation of Neuroscientific Foundations: ......................................................80

CHAPTER TEN ...................................................82

Personal And Professional Growth .....................82

Reflections On The Therapist's Journey ..............82

    1. Reflexivity and self-awareness:......................82

    2. Accepting Vulnerability:.................................83

    3. Empathy and objectivity in Balance: ..............84

**Continuing Education And Skill Development** ........84

    **1. Lifelong Education:** ...........................84

    **2. Peer Consultation and Supervision:**.................85

    **3. Introducing New Methods:** ............................85

**Staying Inspired In Narrative Practice** .....................86

    **1. Plans for Personalized Professional Development:**........................................................86

    **2. Customer Success Stories:**.............................86

    **3. Participating in Community:**..........................87

**Conclusion**................................................................88

**THE END**...................................................................91

# INTRODUCTION

Narrative therapy is a kind of psychotherapy that focuses on people's life stories. Narrative therapy, which was developed in the late twentieth century by Michael White and David Epston, is based on the premise that people build their worlds via the stories they create and tell. It arose in opposition to previous therapy techniques that often pathologized persons and highlighted the therapist's role as an expert.

Narrative therapy is collaborative and non-pathologizing at its foundation. Therapists who work under this paradigm regard their clients as the writers of their own stories, and they strive to assist them in exploring and re-authoring those narratives in a manner that fosters empowerment and positive transformation. Deconstructing problematic tales, discovering alternate views, and recreating more acceptable narratives are all part of the therapeutic process.

Externalization, or isolating the individual from the issue, is a key tenet of narrative therapy, as is the use of "thickening" and "re-authoring" procedures. Externalization allows people to see their problems as apart from their identity, allowing them to obtain a more objective viewpoint. Thickening is the process of examining and enhancing the specifics of someone's story to show the complexity and subtleties, while re-authoring is the process of creating new, more powerful narratives.

One of narrative therapy's benefits is its cultural sensitivity and inclusion. The approach acknowledges the effect of social and cultural discourses on individual tales and emphasizes the significance of evaluating several points of view. Furthermore, story therapy may be used in a variety of situations, including individual, family, and group settings.

Collaboration, curiosity, and respect for the client's knowledge in their own life define the therapeutic partnership in narrative therapy. Therapists often ask open-ended questions, actively listen, and collaborate with clients to explore and modify their narratives.

Overall, story therapy offers a unique and beneficial method of dealing with personal and relationship difficulties. This therapy concept allows people to become the writers of their tales by stressing the power of storytelling and the potential to transform one's narrative, facilitating positive development and personal growth.

# CHAPTER ONE

## Unraveling The Tapestry Of Narrative Therapy

### Embracing The Narrative Paradigm

Narrative Therapy is a therapy method that focuses on the tales people tell about their lives. This paradigm acknowledges that the narratives we make build and interpret human experience. Individuals are seen as active storytellers who actively shape and provide meaning to their experiences. This chapter dives into the narrative paradigm's key concepts and examines how it has evolved into a guiding framework for therapeutic practice.

The narrative paradigm is based on the concept that our identities and realities are changeable and impacted by the tales we tell ourselves and others. Therapists working under this paradigm work with clients to investigate, comprehend, and recreate the narratives that form their lives. Clients may obtain insight into how their tales may be impacting their thoughts, feelings, and actions by doing so.

## Historical Roots And Evolution

It is necessary to trace the historical origins and development of Narrative Therapy to completely comprehend its underpinnings.

The roots of this therapy method may be traced back to postmodern philosophy and social constructionist theories. As therapists and researchers explored alternatives to conventional, pathology-focused theories of psychotherapy in the late twentieth century, the story perspective rose to prominence.

Postmodernism questioned the concept of objective reality and the idea of a single, universal truth. This conceptual change had an impact on the area of psychotherapy, resulting in techniques that recognized the subjective and socially created aspects of human experience. As a result, Narrative Therapy arose as a reaction to the need for therapeutic paradigms that valued diversity, cultural context, and human agency.

## Theoretical Foundations

Narrative Therapy's theoretical roots are firmly entrenched in social constructionism and postmodern philosophy. According to social constructionism, reality is co-constructed via social interactions and language rather than being an intrinsic aspect of the external world. This viewpoint is consistent with the Narrative Therapy idea that people actively shape and interpret their experiences by the tales they tell.

Two significant players in the creation of Narrative Therapy, Michael White and David Epston, highlighted the significance of language and the power dynamics implicit in the tales we tell. White pioneered the notion of "externalizing the problem," a strategy for distancing people from the challenges they encounter, allowing for a more objective examination of the problem's influence on their lives.

Furthermore, the narrative therapist sees therapy as a collaborative process in which both the client and the therapist participate in the co-construction of alternative narratives. This collaborative approach helps clients to write their tales, fostering a feeling of empowerment and self-determination.

Finally, the first chapter of this Narrative Therapy inquiry highlights the paradigm's acceptance of the narrative character of human experience. Practitioners and researchers alike gain insight into the growth of this therapeutic technique and its transformational potential for persons wishing to rewrite the narratives that define their lives by studying its historical origins and theoretical basis.

# CHAPTER TWO

The Power Of Storytelling

Understanding Narratives

Narratives serve as the foundation for our knowledge of the world and ourselves. Stories in the framework of narrative therapy are more than just recounts of events; they are essential to the formation of meaning. People interpret and perceive their experiences by the tales they tell themselves. These tales influence how people make meaning of their lives, relationships, and issues.

Narratives are neither static nor objective; they are fluid and changeable.

Understanding narratives entails acknowledging that people can rewrite their tales. As a therapeutic method, narrative therapy invites clients to investigate and question prevailing narratives that may be confining or limiting them. Individuals may get fresh ideas, perspectives, and a feeling of agency over their lives by deconstructing and rebuilding their stories.

## Narrative Identity And Self-Construction

The theory behind narrative identity is that our sense of self is closely linked to the tales we tell about ourselves. These tales include not just our own experiences, but also the roles we perform, the connections we make, and the cultural scripts we adhere to. In narrative therapy, the therapist works with the client to examine and comprehend the narratives that shape their sense of self.

Recognizing the impact of these narratives on one's beliefs, values, and actions is part of the self-construction process. Clients are urged to critically analyze the tales that may be defining their identity in ways that are inconsistent with their desired goals or objectives. Individuals may actively participate in the rebuilding of their identity in this way, producing a more real and meaningful sense of self.

# Cultural And Social Influences On Storytelling

Narratives are not created in a vacuum; they are profoundly ingrained in cultural and social circumstances. Individuals may use cultural narratives to understand their role in society, shape their expectations, and influence their actions. The scripts that individuals follow in their life tales are influenced by social conventions and expectations.

Cultural and social influences are seen as important components in the formation of tales in narrative therapy. Therapists collaborate with clients to investigate how social myths affect their lives and well-being. Understanding the power dynamics implicit in these narratives and finding strategies to dispute or renegotiate them is part of the process.

Individuals might obtain insight into the external factors creating their tales by identifying and critically assessing cultural and social influences. This understanding enables clients to take a more deliberate and empowered approach to storytelling, allowing them to match their tales with their beliefs and objectives.

Finally, the strength of narrative therapy comes in its potential to affect perceptions, establish identity, and impact behavior. Individuals may recover agency over their tales by comprehending and actively interacting with narratives, enabling personal development and change. Therapists play an important role in aiding this process by fostering a collaborative environment in which clients may examine, criticize, and rebuild the narratives that define their lives.

# CHAPTER THREE

## Narrative Therapy Techniques And Tools

Narrative therapy is a collaborative and empowering technique that focuses on people's life stories. Chapter Three looks into fundamental narrative therapy approaches and tools, emphasizing the need for externalizing issues, reauthoring tales, recognizing unique results and exceptions, successfully employing questions, and evaluating cultural and societal impacts on storytelling.

## Externalizing Problems

Externalizing difficulties, or disconnecting people from their problems, is a core notion in narrative therapy.

Clients acquire a fresh perspective by externalizing the issue, minimizing the feeling of personal failure or identity-related to the situation. Rather of saying, "I am depressed," try, "I am experiencing depression."" This language change enables people to see issues as external things that can be evaluated and dealt with objectively.

Externalization enables a more productive and less stigmatized investigation of the issue, generating a feeling of agency and making it easier to identify distinct outcomes.

Reauthoring entails reconstructing personal narratives. It challenges dominant or negative tales and encourages people to rewrite their stories in ways that reflect their beliefs and objectives. Clients may explore alternate viewpoints while stressing their strengths, resilience, and positive parts of their identity via this approach.

Therapists help clients discover crucial periods in their lives when alternative narratives may be offered, allowing for a more empowered and positive view of their life experiences. Reauthoring narratives may help clients gain agency and take responsibility for their tales.



The discovery of unique outcomes and exceptions to mainstream problem-saturated tales is emphasized in narrative therapy. Therapists help clients identify times when the issue was less prominent or absent, challenging the belief that the condition defines their whole experience.

Individuals get insight into their strengths, coping strategies, and possible solutions by investigating these exceptions. This process promotes the notion that there are times when the issue has less of an impact, fostering a feeling of optimism and possibilities for change.

## The Use Of Questions In Narrative Practices

In narrative therapy, questions play an important role in leading the therapeutic discourse and allowing clients to delve further into their experiences and viewpoints. Open-ended inquiries promote contemplation, while circular questions investigate the connections between different components of the client's story.

Reflective and scaling questions help people assess the severity and effect of issues and solutions, promoting self-awareness and goal planning. The use of questions skillfully enriches the therapeutic process by encouraging participation and co-authorship of the client's story.

## Influences Of Culture And Society On Storytelling

In narrative therapy, it is critical to understand the cultural and social backdrop. People's tales about themselves, their identities, and their relationships are shaped by cultural influences. Therapists must be culturally competent and aware of how cultural narratives influence an individual's perception of their experiences.

Exploring cultural and social factors also assists therapists in appreciating the variety of storytelling styles and standards. This understanding enables a more inclusive and courteous therapy approach that takes into account the larger environment in which clients develop their narratives.

Finally, Chapter Three provides critical narrative therapy approaches and tools that enable people to modify their stories. Externalizing issues, reauthoring narratives, investigating unique results, successfully using inquiries, and identifying cultural influences all contribute to a collaborative and transformational therapy process. These strategies not only help people navigate difficulties, but they also promote resilience, self-discovery, and the co-creation of more positive and empowered life narratives.

# CHAPTER FOUR

## Conversations That Heal

Chapter Four: "Conversations that Heal" delves into the tremendous influence of therapeutic discourse on the process of healing and change in the area of Narrative Therapy. This chapter dives into important principles that drive the therapeutic journey, with a particular emphasis on therapeutic discourse, intentional listening, and the collaborative process of co-creating new narratives.

## The Therapeutic Dialogue

The therapeutic conversation, a sophisticated ballet of words and meaning that evolves between the therapist and the client, is central to Narrative Therapy.

The discourse serves as a dynamic venue for sharing, exploring, and reconstructing tales. In contrast to standard therapy techniques, Narrative Therapy emphasizes language as a strong instrument for understanding and transforming one's environment.

The necessity of providing a secure and nonjudgmental place for therapeutic discourse is emphasized in this chapter. Instead of an expert with predetermined answers, the therapist is seen as a partner who guides the dialog with inquiry and respect. The therapy discourse evolves into a fluid exchange in which the client's feelings and emotions are supported and various viewpoints are examined.

Listening with intention is a cornerstone of Narrative Therapy, and it extends beyond just hearing words. It entails attentive presence, in which the therapist pays close attention to the intricacies of the client's story. This chapter dives into the skill of thoughtful listening, compassionate understanding, and the value of holding one's judgment.

The therapeutic conversation serves as a conduit for the client to express their problems, anxieties, and hopes. The therapist assists the client in making sense of their experiences, seeing patterns, and discovering latent qualities via deliberate listening. The story transforms into a collaborative investigation, establishing a feeling of connection and understanding between therapist and client.

## Co-Creating New Narratives

The transforming practice of co-creating new narratives is at the center of Narrative Therapy. The notion of shifting from problem-saturated to possibility-infused narratives takes center stage in this chapter. The therapist works with the client to question and restructure current tales that may be causing discomfort and constraint.

Therapeutic talks become a channel for empowerment and agency by co-creating new narratives. Clients are encouraged to imagine other stories, reinterpret their roles, and investigate the development of hitherto untapped potentials. The therapist's function shifts to that of a guide, assisting the client in building stories that reflect their values, goals, and preferred modes of being.

The fourth chapter finishes with an examination of the alchemy that happens during therapeutic discussions. The therapeutic conversation, which is founded on active listening and the co-creation of new narratives, catalyzes healing and development. Once burdened by problem-saturated tales, clients begin on a path of self-discovery and agency, eventually rewriting the narratives that define their lives.

Chapter Four exposes the threads of discussions that weave together the fabric of healing, allowing both therapists and clients a shared place for discovery, insight, and the potential of deep transformation in the tapestry of Narrative Therapy.

# CHAPTER FIVE

## Narrative Therapy In Action

Narrative therapy is a kind of psychotherapy that focuses on the tales individuals tell about their lives, acknowledging the power of language in creating and restricting human experience. In Chapter Five, we look at how narrative therapy may be used in practice, looking at case studies and success stories to demonstrate its usefulness. Furthermore, we investigate how this strategy might be developed and utilized in a variety of situations, while simultaneously addressing the obstacles and ethical concerns that therapists may face.

# Case Studies And Success Stories

**1. A Case of Resilience in Narrative Reframing**

We look at how narrative therapy was used to assist a person in reinterpreting their life story in the face of hardship in this case study. The therapist and client worked together to find strengths, resilience, and alternate views by collectively recreating the story.

The success of this instance reveals narrative therapy's transformational potential in allowing people to rewrite their life scripts.

**2. Narrative Interventions and Family Dynamics**

This case study, which examines a family coping with communication breakdowns and conflict, demonstrates how narrative therapy may be used to treat systemic difficulties. Therapists enabled open discussion, promoting understanding, and establishing a more coherent family narrative by addressing family members' individual experiences as well as the family's common story.

**3. Identity Exploration: A Self-Discovery Journey**

In this success story, narrative therapy is used to assist a client in navigating difficulties of identity and self-discovery. The client acquired insights into their values, beliefs, and goals via a collaborative examination of personal narratives, resulting in a more genuine and congruent sense of self.

## Applications In Different Settings

### 1. Fostering Learning Narratives in Educational Settings

Investigate how narrative therapy approaches may be used in educational settings to address difficulties such as student motivation, identity development, and academic obstacles. Case studies demonstrate how storytelling may be used to empower students and provide a pleasant learning environment.

## 2. Redefining Professional Narratives in the Workplace

Examine how story therapy may be used in the workplace to handle workplace issues, improve team relationships, and promote professional growth. Real-world examples show how narrative interventions may help to foster a more pleasant and collaborative workplace culture.

## 3. Empowering Collective Narratives Through Community-Based Initiatives

Investigate the use of story therapy in community contexts to address communal issues and create social change. Case studies demonstrate how storytelling may be used to mobilize communities, develop resilience, and challenge prevailing narratives.



**1. Neutrality and Advocacy in Balance**

Discuss the ethical implications of narrative therapy, including the contradiction between therapist neutrality and social justice advocacy. Address the difficulties that therapists may have while negotiating the underlying value conflicts and power dynamics of the therapeutic process.

**2. In Group Situations, Confidentiality**

Investigate the problems of preserving anonymity when participants share personal histories in group therapy settings. Discuss ways to maintain a feeling of community and mutual support while respecting privacy.

### 3. Cultural Awareness and Diversity

Consider the significance of cultural competency in narrative therapy, taking into account the variety of clients' origins. Discuss cultural sensitivity issues and techniques for ensuring that therapy treatments respect and appreciate the diversity of individual and group cultural narratives.

Finally, Chapter Five gives a thorough examination of story therapy in action, demonstrating its efficacy via case studies and success stories.

It emphasizes the adaptability of this technique in many circumstances while also addressing the ethical issues and problems that therapists must negotiate to work responsibly and effectively.

# CHAPTER SIX

## Collaborative Approaches In Narrative Therapy

Narrative therapy is an approach that emphasizes cooperation as a foundation for therapeutic development. In Chapter Six, we examine the critical role that cooperation plays within the framework of narrative therapy, with a particular emphasis on its influence on transformation. This chapter delves into the role of families and support networks in the narrative therapy process, as well as the significance of multidisciplinary teamwork.

**1. Narratives in Common:**

Individuals are seen as participants in a wider network of connections and social situations in narrative therapy, rather than as separate entities. In narrative therapy, collaborative techniques include the production of shared narratives. Therapists collaborate with clients to co-create new tales that challenge problem-centered narratives. Clients are enabled to reframe their identities and experiences by co-creating alternative tales.

**2. Power Relationships:**
Collaboration in narrative therapy addresses power issues that are common

in conventional therapeutic partnerships. Therapists strive to create egalitarian relationships in which the client's voice is not only heard but also actively impacts the therapy process. This collaborative approach is critical in instilling a feeling of agency and empowerment in clients as they traverse the transformation path.

**3. Externalizing Issues:**

Collaboration includes the practice of externalizing difficulties, which is an important method in narrative therapy. Clients obtain a greater perspective on the challenges they confront by detaching the problem from the individual and collectively assessing its effect. This collaborative externalization approach reduces the impact of the issue and allows customers to see difficulties as distinct entities that can be handled and transformed.

## Involving Families And Support Systems

**1. Systemic Viewpoint:**

Individuals are interrelated throughout their family and societal networks, according to narrative therapy. In Chapter Six, we look at how incorporating families and support networks may improve the therapeutic process. Engaging family members collaboratively provides for a more thorough grasp of the client's experience and the influence of familial dynamics on their narrative.

**2. Rewriting Family Stories:**

Therapists collaborate with families to re-author communal narratives. The emphasis switches from problem-saturated tales to narratives that stress strengths, resilience, and positive elements of relationships by reframing and rebuilding family history. This coordinated effort aids in the transformation of the family system.

**3. Considerations for Culture:**
Cultural elements within family and support networks are also addressed via collaborative methods. Therapists comprehend the cultural background by

allowing clients to share their cultural narratives. By bringing cultural strengths and beliefs into narrative interactions, this collaborative discovery not only respects variety but also improves the therapeutic process.

## Interdisciplinary Collaboration

**1. Holistic Treatment:**

To provide comprehensive treatment, narrative therapy understands the need for multidisciplinary teamwork. This requires collaboration between therapists and specialists from a variety of fields, including psychology, social work, and healthcare. Collaboration ensures a thorough grasp of clients' requirements, allowing for a more nuanced and successful therapeutic approach.

**2. Information Exchange:**

Interdisciplinary cooperation allows professionals to share information and thoughts more easily. This collaborative interaction guarantees that all parties engaged are well-informed about the client's story, allowing for a coordinated and integrated approach to addressing different aspects of the client's life.

**3. Treatment Strategy:**

Collaboration between story therapists and other specialists is essential for building comprehensive treatment strategies. Therapists may adapt treatments to address both the individual and systemic components of the client's difficulties by incorporating knowledge from several disciplines. This cooperative approach improves the overall efficacy of treatment approaches.

Finally, Chapter Six focuses on the transforming impact of cooperation in narrative therapy. The focus on collaboration is fundamental to the process of co-creating narratives that empower people, deepen relationships, and encourage real transformation, whether inside the therapeutic dyad, with families, or via multidisciplinary collaboration.

# CHAPTER SEVEN

## Integrating Cultural Competence

Narrative Therapy is a technique that values cultural competency in its implementation. The emphasis in Chapter Seven switches to the incorporation of cultural sensitivity within the framework of Narrative Therapy.

This chapter discusses the need to address diversity and inclusion, as well as the necessity to customize therapeutic techniques to various cultural situations.

# Cultural Sensitivity In Narrative Therapy

**1. Recognizing Cultural Sensitivity:**

• Cultural sensitivity in Narrative Therapy entails a greater knowledge of and respect for clients' different cultural origins. Therapists must be sensitive to cultural identity, beliefs, values, and traditions.

**2. Opportunities and Challenges:**

• Recognizing the difficulties that cultural differences might offer in treatment is critical. Language hurdles, different cultural standards, and differences in communication styles are examples of these problems.

However, the chapter also looks at how cultural variety might be used to improve therapeutic talks.

**3. Intersectionality:**

• When imbued with cultural awareness, narrative therapy understands the intersections of identity. Therapists investigate how different parts of an individual's identity, such as race, ethnicity, gender, and sexuality, interact and impact their lived experiences and narratives.

## Addressing Diversity And Inclusivity

**1. Cultural Competence Education:**
• Therapists are urged to participate in cultural competency training to improve

their awareness of other cultures. This training provides them with the information and skills they need to manage cultural differences and establish a therapeutic atmosphere that is welcoming to everyone.

**2. Including Cultural Narratives:**

• It is critical to include cultural narratives in the therapy process. Clients' experiences are contextualized within their cultural settings, helping therapists to grasp the varied problems and strengths that come with different origins.

**3. Exploration in Collaboration:**
• Narrative Therapy promotes therapist-client communication. This partnership, in the context of cultural diversity, entails

investigating the influence of cultural narratives on the client's self-perception and relationships.

## Tailoring Approaches To Cultural Contexts

**1. Formalization of Culture:**

• Therapists use cultural formulation to better grasp the cultural elements that shape their clients' experiences. This includes investigating cultural norms, stresses, and the impact of cultural systems on the client's identity.

**2. Genograms of Culture:**
• The chapter introduces the notion of cultural genograms, which are tools that graphically reflect a client's cultural

background, such as family history, customs, and cultural influences. This tool may help you understand the intergenerational effects of cultural narratives.

**3. Technique Flexibility:**

• Narrative Therapy offers therapeutic method versatility. Therapists are urged to tailor their techniques to the client's cultural preferences and beliefs. This adaptability promotes a more customized and successful treatment procedure.

Finally, Chapter Seven emphasizes the significance of incorporating cultural competency into Narrative Therapy. Therapists may establish a more inclusive and successful therapy environment by encouraging cultural awareness, addressing diversity and inclusion, and adjusting techniques to cultural circumstances. This integration not only honors the diversity of multiple narratives but also improves therapy results for clients from diverse cultural backgrounds.

# CHAPTER EIGHT

## Narrative Therapy And Trauma

Narrative therapy is a treatment method that focuses on the stories people tell about their lives and how those stories form their identities and experiences.

In the context of trauma, story therapy may be an extremely effective technique for assisting people in making sense of their horrific experiences, redefining their identities, and working toward healing and recovery.

chapter delves into the intersection of narrative therapy and trauma, with a focus on trauma-informed narrative practices, resilience, post-traumatic development, and trauma narrative case studies.

## Trauma-Informed Narrative Practices

Understanding the enormous influence that trauma may have on an individual's life is required for trauma-informed storytelling techniques. Trauma-informed practitioners understand the ubiquity of trauma, acknowledge its consequences, and establish a safe and supportive therapy environment. In narrative therapy, this entails investigating and recreating the tales people tell about their traumatic experiences jointly.

The following are essential components of trauma-informed storytelling practices:

1. Establishing a feeling of safety and trust is critical when dealing with trauma survivors. Narrative therapists establish a secure environment in which people may share their experiences without fear of being judged.

2. **Externalizing the issue:** Narrative therapy often includes externalizing the issue, which allows patients to see the trauma as distinct from their inner identity. This aids in the reduction of feelings of guilt and self-blame that often accompanies traumatic situations.

3. **Reauthoring the Narrative:** Reauthoring the narrative collaboratively entails assisting folks in reconstructing their tales in a manner that empowers them.

This might involve emphasizing moments of perseverance, strength, and survival rather than concentrating entirely on the terrible experience.

**4. Cultural Sensitivity:** It is important to recognize and respect the individual's cultural setting. Cultural narratives have a tremendous impact on how people comprehend and react to trauma.

## Resilience And Post-Traumatic Growth

As people manage their traumatic experiences, narrative therapy stresses the significance of resilience and post-traumatic development. The capacity to adapt effectively in the face of adversity is referred to as resilience, and post-traumatic development refers to the beneficial psychological changes that may occur as a consequence of trauma.

Resilience and post-traumatic development are fostered in the framework of story therapy by:

1. **Identifying Strengths:** Narrative therapists collaborate with clients to uncover and enhance their strengths, resources, and coping methods.

2. **Reframing problems:** Narrative therapy, by encouraging a change in viewpoint, assists people in reinterpretting problems as opportunities for development and learning.

**3. Creating a Preferred Narrative:** Creating a preferred narrative is imagining a future tale that corresponds with the individual's beliefs, ambitions, and objectives, instilling hope and purpose.

## Case Examples Of Trauma Narratives

Case studies demonstrating the use of narrative therapy in trauma give insight into the transformational potential of storytelling. These instances demonstrate how, with the help of a narrative therapist, people may rebuild their narratives and recover meaning and agency in the aftermath of trauma.

**1. Surviving Domestic abuse:** In this example, a domestic abuse victim collaborates with a narrative therapist to investigate and recreate her story. She starts to perceive herself as a survivor rather than a victim after externalizing the issue and emphasizing her resilience.

**2. A Combat Veteran's Journey:** A combat veteran suffering from post-traumatic stress disorder (PTSD) works with a narrative therapist to rewrite his story. The therapist assists him in integrating his experiences into a larger narrative of personal progress, recognizing the difficulties while stressing his strength and bravery.

**3. Childhood Trauma and Resilience:** A person who has experienced childhood trauma seeks narrative therapy to reframe their story. They learn to perceive themselves as a person who have overcome hardship rather than a product of their traumatic past by externalizing the effect of trauma and highlighting their path of resilience.

Finally, the confluence of narrative therapy and trauma provides people with a narrative-informed lens through which they may make sense of their experiences, discover strength and resilience, and develop narratives that promote their healing and growth. Trauma-informed storytelling methods, an emphasis on resilience, and case studies give a complete knowledge of the therapy process's potential for transformational change.

# CHAPTER NINE

## Research And Advances In Narrative Therapy

Narrative therapy, a therapeutic method that focuses on the stories people tell about their lives, has changed throughout time as a result of continuing research, novel tools, and a continual examination of future paths in the discipline. This chapter digs into current research results, narrative approach advancements, and projected future advances in story therapy.

## Current Research Findings

**1. Narrative Therapy and Neuroscience:**
Recent research has looked at the neurological foundations of narrative therapy, specifically how the brain

interprets and integrates story events. Neuroscientific research has shed light on the effects of narrative on brain function, emotional control, and identity development. Understanding these neurological pathways helps to improve the therapeutic use of story approaches.

**2. Adaptation to Culture and Effectiveness:**

Researchers have looked at the cultural relevance and effectiveness of story therapy in a variety of groups. The research focuses on how to adapt storytelling strategies to diverse cultural settings and how cultural elements impact the therapeutic process. This study adds to continuing attempts to make story therapy more inclusive and successful for a diverse variety of clients.

**3. Specific Population Efficacy:**

A growing amount of research is being conducted to investigate the efficacy of story therapy in various groups such as children, adolescents, couples, and those suffering from trauma or mental health conditions. This study not only demonstrates the adaptability of storytelling tactics but also offers evidence-based ideas on adapting treatments for various demographic groups.

**1. Integration of Digital and Technological Resources:**

The integration of digital tools and technology is one example of story therapy innovation. To improve the therapeutic process, therapists are investigating the use of virtual reality, internet platforms, and interactive storytelling applications. These developments bring up new avenues for reaching out to customers in various situations and harnessing technology for innovative story interventions.

**2. Integrating Expressive Arts with Narrative:**

Narrative therapy has gained popularity in conjunction with expressive arts such as music, visual arts, and theater. Therapists are experimenting with novel approaches to include expressive arts in narrative therapies, allowing clients to express themselves and explore new possibilities.

**3. Practices of Collaborative Narrative:**

Narrative therapy innovations emphasize collaborative techniques in which therapists and clients co-create narratives. This departure from the typical expert-client interaction fosters a feeling of shared authorship in the therapeutic process.

Clients may actively construct their narratives and take control of their experiences via collaborative methods.

## Future Directions In The Field

**1. Positive Psychology Integration:**

The future of story therapy might include a greater incorporation of positive psychology ideas. Research and practice might look at how storytelling approaches can help people not only deal with obstacles and issues, but also improve their strengths, resilience, and personal development.

**2. Globalization and Cultural Sensitivity:**

As story therapy spreads over the world, future approaches will include a greater emphasis on cultural responsiveness. Researchers may investigate how story strategies might be adapted to different cultural settings, and practitioners may stress the value of cultural narrative comprehension in the therapeutic process.

**3. Further Investigation of Neuroscientific Foundations:**

Future studies will most likely focus on the interaction of neuroscience and narrative therapy. Understanding how narrative processes alter brain circuits and contribute to psychological well-being might help to shape more focused and successful therapeutic approaches.

To summarize, the landscape of story therapy is dynamic, with continuing research giving light on its effectiveness, advances broadening its methodologies, and future directions impacting the field's progress. As narrative therapy evolves and evolves, therapists and researchers alike are ready to explore new frontiers in understanding and utilizing the power of tales for healing and change.

# CHAPTER TEN

## Personal And Professional Growth

Chapter Ten dives into the diverse terrain of personal and professional development for therapists in the context of Narrative Therapy. Within the framework of Narrative Practice, this chapter emphasizes the necessity of constant self-reflection, education, skill development, and the nurturing of inspiration.

## Reflections On The Therapist's Journey

**1. Reflexivity and self-awareness:**

• Narrative therapists go on a path of self-discovery. It is essential to understand one's narratives, prejudices, and personal experiences. This introspective approach allows therapists to become more aware of their responses, preconceptions, and countertransference, resulting in a more genuine therapeutic connection.

**2. Accepting Vulnerability:**

• Therapists understand the importance of vulnerability in the therapeutic connection. Sharing personal insights sparingly may strengthen connection and demonstrate openness, fostering a collaborative environment in which both the therapist and the client participate in the narrative re-authoring process.

**3. Empathy and objectivity in Balance:**

• It is critical to strike a balance between sympathetic participation and professional neutrality. The capacity of the therapist to negotiate their emotional reactions while being attentive to the client's needs adds to a therapeutic partnership founded on trust and mutual respect.

## Continuing Education And Skill Development

**1. Lifelong Education:**

• Narrative therapists embrace a culture of lifelong learning. This includes maintaining current treatment techniques, developing research, and important domains such as psychology, sociology, and neuroscience.

**2. Peer Consultation and Supervision:**

• Regular supervision and peer consultation offer therapists with useful feedback, advice, and collaborative problem-solving possibilities. Engaging with coworkers creates a supportive network, which promotes professional development and resilience.

**3. Introducing New Methods:**

• Narrative therapy is a developing profession. Therapists seek and incorporate new approaches, tools, and treatments into their practice regularly.

This adaptable method guarantees that treatment stays dynamic and sensitive to clients' various requirements.

## Staying Inspired In Narrative Practice

**1. Plans for Personalized Professional Development:**

•   Therapists create individualized professional development programs based on their hobbies and areas of interest in narrative therapy. This customized method keeps passion and attention to the practice going.

**2. Customer Success Stories:**
• Drawing inspiration from client success stories strengthens narrative therapy's transforming power.

Celebrating clients' resilience and agency acts as a strong motivation, reminding therapists of the good influence they have on people's lives.

**3. Participating in Community:**

• Narrative therapists are active members of the greater therapeutic community. Participation in conferences, seminars, and professional organizations not only exposes therapists to new viewpoints, but also revitalizes their spirits via shared experiences and collective learning.

Finally, Chapter Ten emphasizes the dynamic and ever-changing aspect of the narrative therapist's journey. Therapists construct a rich and rewarding professional practice that constantly grows to suit the different needs of their clients via self-reflection, continued education, skill development, and a dedication to remaining motivated.

## Conclusion

Narrative Therapy, a kind of psychotherapy that focuses on divorcing people from their issues by recreating their narrative, has a strong and transforming impact. Its focus on the tales we tell about our lives and experiences allows for a change in perspective, allowing people to become the writers of their own stories.

Finally, the heart of Narrative Therapy is its collaborative and courteous approach, which allows patients to externalize their troubles and see them as different entities from themselves. This therapy methodology helps people to recognize strengths, reframe their identities, and discover new ways of interacting with their experiences by deconstructing prevailing narratives and exploring alternate views.

The focus on language, context, and social factors in Narrative Therapy allows for a more in-depth understanding of how our tales form our reality. Individuals may regain agency and create a more empowered and preferable way of life by discovering and reauthoring these narratives.

Finally, Narrative Therapy fosters a feeling of agency, resilience, and empowerment, providing a remarkable potential for personal development and transformation. Its concepts may continue to lead people in their lives by understanding the power of storytelling and appreciating the diversity of storylines that reside inside each of us.

# THE END

www.ingramcontent.com/pod-product-compliance
Lightning Source LLC
Chambersburg PA
CBHW050651250726
48662CB00002B/603